Café Mima

Cuban Cookbook
(Cocina Cubana)

Yoly N. Pérez

I wish to dedicate this cookbook to the memory of my grandmother, Dorinda, who owned Café Mima in Cuba and with her patience and love taught her daughters, my sister, my brother, and me the enjoyment and pleasures of cooking and savoring Cuban food; to my parents, Yolanda and Ramon, for always teaching and maintaining Cuban cultures and values while providing us with an infinite amount of love, affection and understanding; to my Aunts for their recipe contribution and warm kitchens; and to my family and friends for their continued support and encouragement. Thank you and I'll treasure all the memories and love forever.

All my love,
Yoly

History of Café Mima Cuban Cookbook

Born in Havana, Cuba on December 25, 1964, I came to the United States at the early age of three. I have never been back to Cuba. Yet, thanks to my parents, I hold in importance my roots, traditions and values.

From my childhood, I recall waking up to the aroma of Cuban coffee brewing. The smell alone can provide energy – not to mention what it does to you if you have a sip. A traditional Cuban breakfast consists of toasted Cuban bread and Café con Leche with lots of sugar. The Cuban kitchen forms, without a doubt, the nucleus of the family. If you visit someone's home you are expected to taste (if even a bite), if more - consume (beyond all prospect), whatever is being prepared.

My grandmother Dorinda was from Galicia, Spain, immigrated to Cuba at the age of 16 and opened the family restaurant, Café Mima, at the age of 30. She continued to enjoy it for 31 years. Café Mima was a cozy café with green park benches outside, several tables in the back, and an eat-in bar counter at the front. The café's large garage-like front doors opened for breakfast and lunch - allowing the aroma to seep out onto the streets. The gathering of these recipes began when I was a child. I have now compiled and translated them in order to share this wonderful heritage and cuisine. These recipes are but a sampling of the many recipes in my family's collection.

Lots of love, affection and patience make a person whole and are also the perfect ingredients for a scrumptious meal.

Buen Provecho (ENJOY YOUR MEAL!!)

Dedico este libro de cocina a la memoria de mi abuela, Dorinda, dueña de Café Mima en Cuba, que con su paciencia y amor enseño a sus hijas, a mi hermana, a mi hermano, y a mi el gusto y placer de cocinar y difrutar la comida Cubana; a mis padres, Yolanda y Ramón, por siempre procurar y mantener los valores y costumbres Cubanos, así como darnos mucho amor, cariño y comprensión; a mis tías por su contribución de recetas y cocina siempre tan llena de amor; y a mi familia y amistades por su apoyo continuo. Gracias, mantendré el amor y las memorias como un tesoro para siempre.

Con todo mi amor,
Yoly

Historia de el Libro de Cocina Café Mima

Nací en la Habana, Cuba el 25 de Diciembre de 1964 y vine a los Estados Unidos a los tres años de edad. Nunca he regresado a Cuba, pero gracias a mis padres mantengo un arraigo en mis raíces, valores y tradiciones.

Desde que yo era niña recuerdo despertarme con el olor del café Cubano hirviendo, el cual te llena de vida sin mencionar lo que hace si lo pruebas. El desayuno tradicional Cubano es Café con Leche con mucha azúcar y pan cubano con mantequilla. El olor me sigue dando un sentido acojedor y comfortable. Para la mayoría de los Cubanos la cocina es el núcleo de la familia y si estas de visita tienes que probar la comida.

Mi abuela Dorinda nació en Galícia España pero inmigro a Cuba a la edad de 16 años y a la edad de 30 años abrió el restaurante Café Mima el cual tuvo por 31 años. Café Mima era un restaurante acojedor con bancas verdes afuera, mesas en la parte trasera y una barra al frente. Las puertas se abrían para el desayuno y el almuerzo permitiendo que el aroma saliera hacia la calle. Siempre me ha fascinado el arte de la cocina, y mientras que mi abuela y mi mamá cocinaban, yo siendo niña escribí las recetas y años después empece a escribir y traducir este libro que ahora comparto con ustedes. Espero que este libro enriquesca su conocimiento de las tradiciones y comida Cubana. Esta son algunas de la recetas.

El amor, el cariño y la pacienca hace a una persona completa y forman los perfectos ingredientes para una comida sabrosa.

Buen Provecho !!

A Special Thanks To :
Un Especial Agradecimiento A:

Kenneth Bryan

Miguel Cubiles

Fran Fauntleroy

Gonzalo Gorraez

Deborah Hauptmann

Rita Mills

Carolyn Wilson

PAINTING ON COVER "DIALOGO GUAJIRO, 1998" (118˝ x 150˝)
BY WORLD RENOWNED CUBAN ARTIST
Miguel Cubiles

ILUSTRACION DE LA PORTADA "DIALOGO GUAJIRO, 1998" (300cm x 380cm)
POR EL GRAN MAESTRO CUBANO
Miguel Cubiles

Sra. Dorinda Martínez de Ferrero
My grandmother (Mi Abuela)

February 8, 1906 - April 1, 1980
(8 de Febrero 1906 - 1 de Abril 1980)

Table of Contents
(Contenido)

At Café Mima the menu was set up to have one daily special and the a la carte dishes.
(En el Café Mima la carta consistía del especial del día y los platos a la carta).

Caution: Use precaution when using a Pressure cooker. Follow manufacturer instruction and safety requirements.
Precaucion: Al ultilizar la olla de presión, siga las instrucciones y medidas de seguridad del manual del equipo.

Sunday's Special
(Especial del Domingo)

Black Bean Soup (Sopa de Frijoles Negros)

White Rice (Arroz Blanco)

Pork Tenderloin (Carne de Puerco Frita)

Root with Gravy (Yuca con Mojo)

This is the traditional Cuban meal which is typically served
Christmas Eve and on special occasions.

Este plato es la comida tradicional de Nochebuena y ocasiones especiales.

Black Bean Soup
(Sopa de Frijoles Negros)

1 lb. fresh black beans *(frijoles negros)*
1 large bell pepper *(ají)*
10 cups water
⅔ cup olive oil *(aceite oliva)*
1 large onion *(cebolla)*
4 cloves garlic *(dientes de ajo)*
2 large bell peppers *(ají)*
2 tbsps. salt *(sal)*
¼ tsp. pimiento pepper *(pimento rojo)*
¼ tsp. oregano *(orégano)*
1 bay leaf *(laurel)*
1 tsp. sugar *(azúcar)*
4 tsps. dry white wine *(vino seco)*
2 tbsps. vinegar *(vinagre)*
4 tsps. olive oil *(aceite de oliva)*
Salt to taste *(sal al gusto)*

Place the black beans with the water and one large bell pepper (left whole with the inside cleaned out) in a pressure cooker and cook for approximately one hour on medium heat until beans are soft. Purée the garlic, onion, and bell pepper in a food processor. Sauté the mixture in olive oil for a few minutes. Once sautéed, add the sauté to the black bean soup and stir. Add the oregano, salt, pimiento, bay leaf and sugar. Stir well and let cook on medium low for one hour. Add the wine and vinegar and stir well. The black beans should be creamy; if not, let the beans cook a little bit longer. Before serving add two teaspoons of olive oil. Add salt to taste.

Serves 8-10.

Ponga los frijoles con agua y un ají grande en la olla de presión por una hora en un fuego mediano hasta que se ablandan. Pase por el procesador el ají, ajo, y la cebolla y sofrialo en el aceite caliente. Agregue en ese sofrito una taza de los frijoles para que no se sequen. Añadaselo a los otros frijoles y agreguele el oregano, sal, pimienta, laurel y la azúcar. Dejelo cocinar una hora más y despues añadale el vinagre, y el vino seco para que quede bien cuajado. Al momento de servirlo añadale dos cucharadas de aceite de oliva. Añadale sal al gusto.

Da 8-10 raciones.

White Rice
(Arroz Blanco)

1 lb. white rice *(arroz blanco)*
3 cups water *(agua)*
3 tsps. olive oil *(aceite de oliva)*
1 tsp. salt *(sal)*

Heat the olive oil in a pot and add the water and salt. When the water starts to boil, immediately add the rice. Allow the water to boil then reduce heat to low. Cook, with the pot covered, for approximately 30 minutes until the rice is tender.

Serves 6-8.

En una cazuela, caliente el aceite de oliva y añadale el agua y la sal. Inmediatamente cuando el agua empiece a hervir, añadale el arroz. Cocine el arroz en fuego lento bien tapado por aproximadamente 30 minutos hasta que el arroz este blando.

Da 6-8 raciones.

Pork Tenderloin
(Carne de Puerco Frita)

2 large packages Pork Tenderloin
  (carne de puerco)
Vegetable oil *(aceite para freir)*
4 limes *(limones)*
4 bitter or sweet oranges *(naranja agria)*
1 onion *(cebolla)*
8 cloves garlic *(dientes de ajo)*
Salt to taste *(sal al gusto)*

Remove all fat from the pork and cut into one inch squares. Marinate the pork with salt, garlic, and the juice of the limes and oranges. Let sit all night. One hour before you are ready to eat, fry the pork tenderloin in the vegetable oil. Make sure the oil is on high to start, and then lower to medium for approximately 25-35 minutes until the pork is well cooked. Once the pork is cooked on the inside, fry it on high to brown the outside. Remove the pork from the oil and set aside. Cut onions in rounds and sauté the onions until tender with a little bit of the oil used for the pork. Place pork on plate and add the sautéed onions to the top of the pork. Note: The pork requires a lot of salt for seasoning. For additional flavor add mojo (see recipe, next page) to the onion mix while sautéing.

Serves 6-8.

Remuevale toda la grasa de la carne de puerco y corte la carne en cuadritos. Sazone la carne con sal, ajo, naranja agria, limones y mojo. Deje reposar toda la noche. Una hora antes de comer, fría la carne en aceite con el fuego primo alto y después en fuego mediano por 25-35 minutos. Cuando el puerco este cocinado suba el fuego alto para dorar la carne. Remueva la carne del aceite y pongala a un lado. Corte la cebolla en ruedas y sofriala con un poco de aceite de donde frió el puerco hasta que la cebolla este mustia. Si tiene mojo agregue un poco al sofrito. (Vea la receta para el mojo en la proxima pagina.) Ponga la carne de puerco en un plato y encima la mezcla de la cebolla.

Da 6-8 raciones.

Root with Gravy
(Yuca con Mojo)

2 lbs. fresh root *(yuca)*
¼ cup olive oil *(aceite de oliva)*
1 onion *(cebolla)*
8 cloves garlic *(dientes de ajo)*
⅛ tsp. pimiento pepper *(pimento rojo)*
Pinch of oregano *(orégano)*
1 bitter orange *(naranja agria)*
2 tbsps. vinegar *(vinagre)*
2 tbsps. parsley *(perejil)*
Salt to taste *(sal al gusto)*

Peel the skin off the yucca and cut the yucca into large squares (approximately 2 inches). Place the yucca in a large pot with water covering the yucca completely and add a bit of salt. Cook the yucca for approximately 20 minutes at medium heat until the yucca is soft. Once the yucca is soft, remove from the heat and pour cold water over it (the cold water will cause the yucca to open a little). Set the yucca aside. Mash the garlic and mix it with the oregano, pimiento pepper, bitter orange, and vinegar. Mix well. In a skillet, heat the olive oil and sauté the finely chopped onion. Once the onion is sautéed, add the garlic mixture and parsley and stir around the skillet a few times (not too long). Place the yucca in a serving dish and pour the mixture over it adding some parsley for decoration.

Serves 6-8.

Pele la yuca y corte en trozos. Se pone a cocinar la yuca en una cazuela donde quede cubierta por el agua y se le agrega la sal. Cocinela al fuego mediano por 20 minutos hasta que este suave la yuca. Cuando ya este bien cocinada se le agrega agua fria a la yuca para que se abra y se saca de la candela. Con un mortero se machacan los ajos. Añada el ajo, orégano, pimienta, naranja agria y vinagre. En un poco de aceite caliente se sofrie la cebolla. Cuando la cebolla ya esta lista se le agrega lo del mortero y el perejil seco.

Da 6-8 raciones.

Monday's Special
(Especial del Lunes)

ChickPea Stew (Potaje de Garbanzo)
Fried Steak (Bistec Empanizado)

This stew may be accompanied with a green salad and Cuban bread (French-like bread).
Este plato se puede acompañar con una ensalada verde y pan cubano (como pan francés).

Chickpea Stew
(Potaje de Garbanzos)

1 lb. fresh chickpeas *(garbanzos)*
1 chorizo
¼ lb. salt pork/bacon *(tocino)*
1 lb. potatoes *(papas)*
1 lb. ham hocks *(lacón)*
½ cup olive oil *(aceite oliva)*
¼ tsp. condiment of yellow coloring *(bijol)*
1 bell pepper *(ají)*
1 onion *(cebolla)*
2 cloves garlic *(dientes de ajo)*
¼ tsp. pimiento pepper *(pimento rojo)*
1 bay leaf *(laurel)*
Salt to taste *(sal al gusto)*

Place the fresh chickpeas with three liters of water in a pot and let sit overnight. The following day, add the ham hocks to the chickpeas and water (that sat overnight) and place in a pressure cooker for approximately one hour (the pressure cooker should be on high until it reaches full pressure and then lowered to medium). Once the chickpeas have softened, add the potatoes chopped into ½ inch squares and continue cooking over medium heat. (If the liquid starts to consume, add more water). Finely chop the bacon and the chorizo and sauté in olive oil until brown. While browning, add the bell pepper, onion, and garlic and continue sautéing. Add the sautéed ingredients into the stew and stir. Add the bay leaves, bijol and pimento. Stir and cook on medium heat until mixture starts to boil and then reduce heat to low or medium low until the stew thickens. Add salt to taste.

Serves 6-8.

Ponga los garbanzos a remojar el día anterior en agua. Al otro día pongalo a cocinar por una hora en la olla de presión. Agregue las papas picadas al potaje y asegurece que no se vaya ha quedar sin agua el caldo. Pique el tocino y el chorizo en pedacitos chiquitos y sofrialo en aceite de oliva. Cuando vea que esta un poco dorado agregue el ají, cebolla, ajo y revuelva el potaje. Continue a cocinarlo en fuego lento añadiendole el pimiento, bijol y el laurel. Cocinelo hasta que este un poco espeso. Añadale sal al gusto.

Da 6-8 raciones.

Fried Steak
(Bistec Empanizado)

1 cup oil *(aceite)*
⅛ tsp. black pepper *(pimienta)*
1 lemon *(limón)*
4 thin breakfast steaks *(bistec de cañada finitos)*
2 garlic cloves *(dientes de ajo)*
1 egg *(huevo)*
1 cup cracker meal or bread crumbs *(galleta molida)*
½ tsp. salt (sal)

Season the steaks with salt, garlic, and lemon juice and let marinate for at least one hour. Whip the eggs and add the black pepper. Dip the steaks in the egg mixture and then dip it in the bread crumbs. Repeat this two to three times. Refrigerate coated steaks for one to two hours. In hot oil, fry the steaks, turning several times. Lower the heat to medium and fry the steaks until fully cooked. Approximate cooking time is 3 to 5 minutes per steak. Remove from oil and serve with red beans and rice or any desired side dish.

Serves 4.

Sazone los bistecs con sal, ajo y el jugo de limón y guárdelos bien tapados en la nevera durante una hora por lo menos. Bata los huevos con la pimienta. Escurra bien los bistecs y páselos por el huevo batido y la galleta molida dos o tres veces. Guárdelos en la nevera por una o dos horas. Fríalos en el aceite caliente volteandolos constantemente hasta que estén doraditos y cocinados.

Da 4 raciones.

Tuesday's Special
(Especial del Martes)

Spanish Stew (Caldo Gallego)

This dish is very filling and can be accompanied with a green salad and Cuban bread (French-like bread).
Este plato es muy fuerte y se puede acompañar con una ensalada verde y pan cubano.

Spanish Stew
(Caldo Gallego)

1½ lbs. fresh lima beans *(judías)*
1 chorizo
½ lb. salt pork/bacon *(tocino)*
1 lb. potatoes *(papas)*
1 lb. ham hocks *(lacón)*
¼ cup olive oil *(aceite oliva)*
¼ lb. lard *(unto)*
1 head cabbage *(berza)*
3 cloves garlic *(dientes de ajo)*
Salt to taste *(sal al gusto)*

Combine the fresh lima beans with the bacon, ham hocks and enough water to fill three quarters of the pot. Pressure cook for one hour. The pressure cooker should be on high and then lowered to medium to prevent the stew from sticking. When the lima beans are soft, add the potatoes, cabbage and chorizo cut into squares and stir over low to medium heat. While the soup is cooking on low, sauté the garlic in a pan with lard. Once the garlic is sautéed, add it to the soup and stir. Cook on low to medium heat for about 20 minutes. Make sure that the stew has enough water; if the liquid starts to evaporate, add more water. The stew should have a creamy consistency. Add salt to taste. Before serving, cut the ham hocks, chorizo and bacon into small pieces.

Serves 6-8.

Ponga las judías con el lacón y el tocino en una cazuela con agua. Cocínelo en la olla de presión por una hora en fuego mediano. Cuando todo este blando, se le agregan las papas picadas en pedazos al igual que la berza y el chorizo. Mientras que esto se cocina en fuego lento, en un sartén con el aceite caliente se pica un pedacito de unto y se sofríe con el ajo machacado. Cuando este frito y se doren los ajos se sacan estos y el resto del sofrito se le agrega al caldo y se cocina por 20 minutos en fuego lento siempre cuidando que no se seque y cocinelo hasta que este un poco espeso. Añadale sal al gusto. Siempre para servirlo se pica el lacón, tocino y chorizos en pedacitos.

Da 6-8 raciones.

Wednesday's Special
(Especial del Miercoles)

Lima Bean Soup (Aluvias)

Ham Croquette (Croqueta de Jamón)

The Ham Croquettes can be served with a green salad, tomatoes and saltine crackers.
Este plato se puede acompañar con una ensalada verde, tomates y galletas de sal.

Lima Bean Soup
(Aluvias)

1 lb. fresh lima beans *(habas limas)*
2 large ham hocks *(lacón)*
½ cup olive oil (aceite oliva)
1 bell pepper *(ají)*
1 onion *(cebolla)*
2 cloves garlic *(dientes de ajo)*
1 can tomato sauce *(salsa de tomate)*
Salt to taste *(sal al gusto)*

In a pressure cooker add the lima beans, ham hocks and enough water to fill approximately three fourths of the pot. Pressure cook on medium heat until the beans are tender - approximately 35 minutes. Remove the beans after allowing the pressure cooker to cool before opening. In heated olive oil, sauté the onion, bell pepper and diced garlic until soft and add tomato sauce. Remove the ham hocks from the soup and cut the ham into bite size pieces and discard the fat. Add the ham and the sautéed onion mixture to the soup and stir. Cook the soup on high until it begins to boil. Stir constantly. Reduce heat to medium and cook for approximately 15 minutes. Add salt to taste and cook for another 5 minutes. If the soup is runny, smash several beans to thicken. If the soup is too thick, add more water while it is cooking. Serve with warm bread.

Serves 6-8.

Ponga a cocinar las habas limas y el lacón en una olla de presión con agua a más de la mitad. Cocinelo a fuego mediano por 35 minutos hasta que las habas limas estén suave. Tenga cuidado en abrir la olla; asegurece que esta fria la olla antes de abrirla. Sofria la cebolla, ají y ajo picadito en el aceite caliente y la salsa de tomate. Remueva el lacón de la sopa y corte el jamón en pedacitos (bote la grasa). Añadale el jamón y la cebolla/aji/ajo/salsa de tomate a la sopa y cocinelo en fuego mediano sin presión por 15 minutos. Añadale sal al gusto y cocine por otros 5 minutos. Cocinelo hasta que este un poco espeso. Si no esta espeso machuque unas cuantas habas limas. Si esta muy espeso añadale más agua. Sirva con pan.

Da 6-8 raciones.

Ham Croquette
(Croqueta de Jamon)

1 lb. finely chopped ground ham
   (jamón molido)
1 tsp. salt *(sal)*
1 onion *(cebolla)*
4 cloves garlic *(dientes de ajo)*
1 stick butter *(mantequilla)*
¼ tsp. nutmeg *(nuez moscada)*
⅛ tsp. black pepper *(pimienta)*
2 cups flour *(harina)*
1 cup milk *(leche)*
5 eggs *(huevos)*
2 cups bread crumbs *(galleta molida)*
Oil *(aceite)*

In a food processor, chop the onion and garlic. Melt one stick of butter in a skillet and add the onion mix, ground ham, nutmeg, salt, and black pepper. Cook on low heat for approximately 10 minutes. Stir constantly to avoid sticking. Mix the flour and milk to form a béchamel sauce. Slowly add the béchamel sauce to the ham sauce at low heat until the ham begins to thicken. Place the ham in a bowl and allow it to come to room temperature. Form a sausage-like shaped croquette with approximately one tablespoon of the ham mixture. Beat the 5 eggs and set aside. Place two cups of bread crumbs in a bowl and set aside. Dip the croquettes in the egg mixture and then the bread crumb mixture (repeat this procedure twice). The croquettes are now ready to be fried. Fry the croquettes in hot oil on medium heat for approximately 5 minutes until they are thoroughly cooked and browned.

Serves 25-30 croquettes.

Muela la cebolla y el ajo. Caliente la mantequilla y sofria la cebolla, ajo, jamón molido, sal, nuez moscada, y pimienta en fuego lento por aproximadamente 10 minutos. Revuelva constantemente. Mezcle la harina con la leche para hacer una salsa bechamel. Añadale la salsa bechmel al jamón en fuego lento revolviendo constantement hasta que tenga espesor la croquetas. Ponga la masa en una fuente y deje enfriar bien la masa por lo menos un par de horas antes de formar las croquetas. Para formar las croquetas tome una cucharada de la masa y formela como una salchicha. Bata los huevos. Envuelva dos veces en huevo batido y galleta molida. Frialas en fuego mediano hasta que estén doraditas.

Da 25-30 Croqueta.

Thursday's Special
(Especial del Jueves)

Chicken and Rice (Arroz con Pollo)

This dish may be accompanied by a dinner salad.
Este plato se puede acompañar con una ensalada verde.

Chicken and Rice
(Arroz con Pollo)

1 large chicken *(un pollo grande)*
1 bell pepper *(ají)*
1 onion *(cebolla)*
3 cloves garlic *(dientes de ajo)*
1 bitter orange *(naranja agria)*
1 can tomato sauce *(pure de tomate)*
½ can pimiento pepper *(pimento rojo)*
1 can peas *(petit pois)*
3 tbsps. salt *(sal)*
⅛ tsp. black pepper (pimienta)
2 bay leaves (laurel)
2½ cups dry white wine *(vino seco)*
2 cups chicken broth *(caldo de pollo)*
1½ lbs. white rice *(arroz blanco)*
1 cup water *(agua)*
¼ tsp. of condiment of yellow coloring
  (bijol)
⅓ cup oil *(aceite)*

Boil a small portion of the chicken in a pot full of water to make chicken broth. Cut up the chicken into edible pieces (thighs, breast, wings etc.) and set aside. Prepare to season by mashing the garlic with the bitter oranges. Pour over the chicken and set aside for an hour. In a food processor, purée onion, bell pepper, and ½ can of pimiento pepper with some of the liquid, salt, black pepper, bay leaf, dry wine, chicken broth, condiment of yellow coloring and water. Mix well in the food processor and set aside. Heat oil and sauté the chicken with the garlic and bitter orange seasoning until browned. Add the ingredients that have been puréed and let the chicken cook well, stirring occasionally. When the chicken is partially cooked, add the rice. Cook on low heat until the rice is cooked. Add most of the peas and stir. Garnish with remainder of peas and pimiento peppers.

Serves 8.

Phaga un caldo con los menudos del pollo. Corte el pollo en pedazos y adobelos con ajo machado y naranja agria una hora antes de empezar a cocinar. Caliente el aceite y dore el pollo. Pase por el procesador la cebolla, el ají, la mitad de la lata de pimientos morrones con un poco de su líquido, agregue la sal, pimienta, las hojas de laurel, el bijol, vino seco, el agua y el caldo. Cuando el pollo este medio cocinado se le agrega el arroz. Déjelo a fuego lento hasta que el grano este abierto y blando. Añada los petit pois. Adórnelo con pimientos and petit pois.

Da 8 raciones.

Friday's Special
(Especial del Viernes)

Beef and Potatoes (Carne con Papas)

This dish may be accompanied by white rice and a dinner salad.
Este plato se puede acompañar con arroz blanco y una ensalada verde.

Beef and Potatoes
(Carne con Papas)

2 lbs. beef tenderloin *(carne de res)*
2 lbs. potatoes *(papas)*
½ cup oil *(aceite)*
⅛ tsp. oregano *(orégano)*
2 cloves garlic *(dientes de ajo)*
1 tsp. pimiento pepper *(pimento rojo)*
¼ tsp. black pepper *(pimienta)*
2 bay leaves *(laurel)*
2 tsps. salt *(sal)*
1 onion *(cebolla)*
2 bell peppers *(ají)*
1 can tomato sauce *(salsa de tomate)*
1 cup dry white wine *(vino seco)*
¼ cup capers *(alcaparras)*
1 cup water *(agua)*

Cut the beef tenderloins into approximately one inch squares and sauté the beef in hot oil. When the beef is begins to brown, add the salt, black pepper, pimiento pepper, bay leaf, garlic, onion (diced) and bell pepper (diced). Allow to cook on low heat for about 15 minutes and then add the tomato sauce, white wine, and water. Cook on low heat until the meat is partially cooked (stirring occasionally) and then add the potatoes (cut into small squares). Cook on low to medium heat until the meat and the potatoes are done. If the liquid starts to evaporate, add a little more water and/or white wine. The beef can be served with white rice if desired.

Serves 6-8.

Corte la carne en cuadraditos. Sofriala en el aceite caliente. Cuando este dorada, añada la sal, pimentón, laurel, pimienta, orégano, la cebolla picadita, los ajos machacados y el ají picadito. Cuando este un poca dorado se le agrega la salsa de tomate, el vino seco, y el agua. Déjelo al fuego lento hasta que la carne este medio cocinada y entonces agregue las papas cortadas en cuadraditos y las alcaparras. Cocine al fuego lento hasta que la carne y la papás este cocinada. Si se seca un poco agreguele un poco mas de agua y vino seco. Este plato se puede servir con arroz blanco.

Da 6-8 raciones.

Saturday's Special
(Especial del Sabado)

Chopped Beef (Picadillo)

White Rice (Arroz Blanco)

This dish may be accompanied with Fried Ripe Bananas and a green salad.
Este plato se puede acompañar con plátanos maduros fritos y una ensalada verde.

Chopped Beef
(Picadillo)

1 lb. ground beef *(carne de res molida)*
½ lb. ground ham *(jamón molido)*
¼ cup oil *(aceite)*
1 bell pepper *(ají)*
1 onion *(cebolla)*
2 cloves garlic *(dientes de ajo)*
¼ cup capers *(alcaparras)*
1 tbsp. salt *(sal)*
⅛ tsp. black pepper *(pimienta)*
1 can tomato sauce *(pure de tomate)*
A pinch of oregano *(pisca de orégano)*
¼ cup dry white wine *(vino seco)*

Heat oil and sauté diced onion, bell pepper and garlic. Cook the ground beef and ground ham until almost done (cook for several minutes), stirring occasionally. Add the onions, bell pepper and garlic halfway through cooking the meat. Add the rest of the ingredients and let cook on low heat for approximately 25 minutes. Serve over white rice.

Serves 6-8.

Caliente el aceite y sofria en la cebolla, ají y ajo picadita. Sofria la carne de res y el jamón molido y cuando este un poco cocinada añadale la cebolla, ají y ajo y deje que cocine unos minutos. Añadale los demás ingredientes y dejelo cocinar a fuego lento unos 25 minutos. Sirvalo con arroz blanco.

Da 6-8 raciones.

White Rice
(Arroz Blanco)

1 lb. white rice(arroz blanco)
3 cups water (agua)
3 tsps. olive oil (aceite de oliva)
1 tsp. salt (sal)

Heat the olive oil in a pot and add the water and salt. When the water starts to boil, immediately add the rice. Allow the water to boil then reduce the heat to low. Cook, with the pot covered, for approximately 30 minutes, until the rice is tender.

Serves 6-8.

En una cazuela, caliente el aceite de oliva y añadale el agua y la sal. Inmediatamente cuando el agua empiece a hervir, añadale el arroz. Cocine el arroz en fuego lento bien tapado por aproximadamente 30 minutos hasta que el arroz este blando.

Da 6-8 raciones.

A La Carte
(A La Carta)

Cuban Sandwich (Sandwich Cubano)
Fried Green Bananas (Plátanos Verdes Fritos)
Fried Ripe Bananas (Plátanos Maduros Fritos)
Potatoes Stuffed with Beef (Papa Rellena)
Shredded Beef (Vaca Frita)
Split Pea Soup (Potaje de Chicharos)
Red Bean Soup (Potaje de Frijoles Colorados)
Rice and Beans (Moros y Cristianos)

All soups may be accompanied by a green salad. Fried bananas may be served with any Cuban dish. Potatoes stuffed with beef may be accompanied by rice/beans and green salad. Shredded Beef can be accompanied with white rice and green salad.

Todas las sopas se pueden acompañar con una ensalada verde. Los plátanos fritos se pueden acompañar con cualquier plato Cubano. La papa rellena se puede acompañar con arroz o arroz y frijoles y una ensalada verde. La vaca frita se puede acompañar con arroz blanco y una ensalada verde.

Cuban Sandwich
(Sandwich Cubano)

Cuban or French bread *(pan cubano o francés)*
1 slice Swiss cheese *(queso suizo)*
2 slices pork *(carne de puerco)*
3 slices ham *(jamón)*
1 slice turkey *(pavo)*
4 slices pickle *(pepino)*
Mustard *(mostaza)*
Butter *(mantequilla)*

Cut the bread approximately 6 inches long and butter both sides with mustard and butter. Add all the ingredients layered in the sandwich. Heat the sandwich on both sides pressing the sandwich together. Remove from skillet and serve.

Serves

Corte el pan approximadamente 6 pulgadas de largo y agregue mantequilla y mostaza al pan. Añadale el resto de los ingredientes. Caliente el sandwich en ambos lados prensándolo. Remueva y sirva caliente.

Da 1 racion.

Fried Green Bananas
(Platanos Verde Fritos)

2 green bananas *(plátanos verdes)*
Vegetable oil *(aceite)*

Peel the bananas and cut rounds approximately ¼ inch in thickness. Heat oil and fry the bananas at low to medium heat until the inside of the banana is cooked. After the inside of the banana is cooked, remove the banana from the oil and place on top of a paper towel. Place another paper towel above the banana. With your fist, mash down on the banana to flatten, and then place it back in the hot oil to continue cooking and browning. Once the banana is cooked and browned, remove from the oil, add a little bit of salt, and serve. Serve as a side dish to any meal.

Serves 6-8

Se pelan los dos plátanos y se pican en ruedas de una pulgada. En aceite caliente, fríen los plátanos en fuego lento hasta que los plátanos estén cocinados por dentro. Saque los plátanos del aceite y aplastelos con la palma de la mano. Se vuelven a freír en aceite caliente para que se cocinen por ambos lados y se doren. Los plátanos pueden acompañar cualquier comida.

Da 6-8 raciones.

Fried Ripe Banana
(Platanos Maduros Fritos)

2 ripe green bananas *(plátanos maduro)*
Vegetable oil *(aceite)*

Peel the skin off the bananas and slice the bananas at an angle about ¼ inch in thickness. Heat oil in a pot and fry the banana pieces until they are cooked and browned. Serve the bananas as a side dish to any meal.

Serves 6-8

Pelar los dos plátanos y se pican en lascas. Se agrega el aceite en un sartén y cuando este el aceite caliente se le agregan los plátanos. Se concinan dejandolos dorar por ambos lados. Los plátanos pueden acompañar cualquier comida.

Da 6-8 raciones.

Potato Stuffed with Ground Beef
(Papa Rellena)

½ lb. ground beef *(carne de res molida)*
1 lb. red potatoes *(papas rojas)*
½ tsp. salt (sal)
½ can tomato sauce *(salsa de tomate)*
1 small onion *(cebolla)*
3 cloves garlic *(dientes de ajo)*
½ tsp. salt *(sal)*
⅛ tsp. black pepper *(pimienta)*
½ stick of butter *(1/2 barra de mantequilla)*
1 small cream cheese *(queso crema)*
4 eggs *(huevos)*
2 cups bread crumbs *(galleta molida)*
Oil *(aceite)*

Peel the potatoes and cut into squares. Boil the potatoes in water with salt until the potato is soft. Mash the potatoes with the butter and cream cheese. Wisk until creamy and set aside. Brown the ground beef on medium heat and drain fat. Add the tomato sauce, chopped onion, garlic, and salt to the ground beef and cook on medium heat for 15 to 20 minutes. Set aside and let the potato and ground beef mix cool. To form the potato place a small amount of the potato in the palm of your hand and fill the center with ground beef. Add more potato to make a ball with meat enclosed. This should be about the size of a baseball. Let the potato balls cool in the refrigerator for one hour. In a bowl, whip the eggs with salt and black pepper. Remove the potatoes from the refrigerator and dip each potato in the egg mixture and then the bread crumbs (do this twice). Fry in hot oil for 5 minutes at medium heat until the potatoes are browned. Oil must cover the entire potato.

Makes 15-20 potato balls.

Pele la papa, corte en cuadrado y hierva las papas en agua con 1 cucharadita de sal en fuego mediano hasta que estén blandas. Mezcle la papa con la mantequilla, queso crema y pongala a un lado. Cocine la carne de res molida en fuego mediano hasta que este bien cocinado. Remuevale la grasa. Corte la cebolla y el ajo finamente. Agregue la salsa de tomate, cebolla, y ajo a la carne de res molida y cocine en fuego mediano por 15- 20 minutos. Deje que se enfrie bien. Para formar la papa rellena, agrega papa en la palma de la mano y ponga la carne en el centro. Forme la papa del tamaño de un pelota de beisbol. Deje enfriar en la nevera por una hora. Bata los huevos con sal y pimienta. Envuelvala dos veces en huevo batido y galleta molida. Frialas en fuego mediano hasta que estén doraditas.

Da 15-20 papas rellenas.

Shredded Beef
(Vaca Frita)

1 lb. flank steak *(falda)*
Olive oil *(aceite oliva)*
1 onion *(cebolla)*
8 cloves garlic *(dientes de ajo)*
1 tsp. salt *(sal)*
½ tsp. black pepper *(pimienta)*
⅛ cup mojo *(mojo)*
2 limes *(limones)*

Place flank steak in a pressure cooker with water to cover half the steak. Cook for about 40 minutes on medium heat or until steak is very tender. Make sure the pressure cooker is cool before opening. Shred the steak by pulling it apart into thread-like pieces. Sauté in olive oil the chopped onion, salt, pepper, and garlic until the onions are soft. Add the shredded steak and cook on medium heat until the steak browns and becomes crispy. Prior to removing the steak, add the mojo and stir well. Squeeze fresh limes over the steak prior to serving.

Serves 4 - 6.

Ponga la falda con agua (a un nivel que este a la mitad de la falda) en la olla de presión por 40 minutos en un fuego mediano hasta que se ablande. Sofria la cebolla picadita, ajo, sal y pimienta en aceite de oliva. Añadaselo a la carne y cocine en fuego mediano hasta que la falda este dorada. Añadale el mojo y revuelva bien. Antes de servir exprima los limones encima de la vaca frita.

Da 4 - 6 raciones.

Split Pea Soup
(Potaje de Chicharos)

1 lb. split peas *(chicharos)*
1 chorizo
¼ lb. salt pork/bacon *(tocino)*
1 lb. potatoes *(papas)*
½ lb. ham hocks *(lacón)*
½ cup olive oil *(aceite de oliva)*
1 bell pepper *(ají)*
1 onion *(cebolla)*
2 cloves garlic *(dientes de ajo)*
¼ tsp. pimiento pepper *(pimento rojo)*
¼ tsp. oregano *(orégano)*
⅛ tsp. black pepper *(pimienta)*
1 bay leaf *(laurel)*
½ can tomato sauce *(pure de tomate)*
2 tbsps. vinegar *(vinagre)*
Salt to taste *(sal al gusto)*

Place the split peas, ham hocks, and three liters of water in a pot and let sit overnight. The next day place in a pressure cooker for approximately one hour (the pressure cooker should be on high until it reaches full pressure and then lowered to medium). Remove the ham hocks and cut the ham into bite size pieces and discard the bone and fat. Once the split peas have softened, add the ham, the potatoes chopped into ½ inch squares, and the chorizo cut into squares. Continue cooking over medium heat. Finely chop the remaining ingredients and sauté in olive oil. Add the sautéed ingredients to the stew and stir. Stir and cook on medium until mixture starts to boil and then lower to low or medium low until the stew thickens. Cook for approximately 20 minutes. Add salt to taste.

Serves 6-8.

Ponga los chicharos y el lacón a remojar el día anterior en tres litros de agua. Al otro día pongalo a cocinar por una hora en la olla de presión. Remueva el lacón y corte el jamón. Bote el hueso y la grasa. Agregue el jamón, las papas picadas y el chorizo picado al potaje. Pique los demás ingredientes en pedacitos chiquitos y sofrialo en aceite de oliva. Agregue el sofrito al potaje. Cocinelo al fuego lento hasta que este un poco espeso. Cocinelo aproximadamente 20 minutos. Añadale sal al gusto.

Da 6-8 raciones.

Red Bean Soup
(Potaje de Frijoles Colorados)

1 lb. red beans *(frijoles colorados)*
1 chorizo
¼ lb. salt pork/bacon *(tocino)*
1 lb. potatoes *(papas)*
½ lb. ham hock *(lacón)*
½ cup olive oil *(aceite de oliva)*
¾ lb. squash *(calabaza)*
1 bell pepper *(ají)*
1 onion *(cebolla)*
2 cloves garlic *(dientes de ajo)*
1 can tomato sauce *(pure de tomate)*
⅛ tsp. black pepper *(pimienta)*
¼ tsp. pimiento pepper *(pimento rojo)*
2 tsps. vinegar *(vinagre)*
1 bay leaf *(laurel)*
Salt to taste

Place the red beans and ham hocks with three liters of water in a pot and let sit overnight. Place in a pressure cooker for approximately one hour (the pressure cooker should be on high until it reaches full pressure and then lowered to medium). After the pressure cooker cools, remove the ham hocks and cut the ham into bite size pieces. Discard the bone and fat. Once the red beans have softened, add the ham, the chorizo cut into squares, and the potatoes chopped into ½ inch squares. Continue cooking over medium heat. Finely chop the remaining ingredients and sauté in olive oil. Add the sautéed ingredients into the stew and stir. Stir and cook on medium until mixture starts to boil. Lower the heat to low or medium low until the stew thickens. Cook for approximately 20 minutes. Add salt to taste.

Serves 6-8.

Ponga los frijoles colorados y el lacón a remojar el día anterior en tres litros de agua. Al otro día póngalo a cocinar por una hora en la olla de presión. Remueva el lacón y corte el jamón. Bote el hueso y la grasa. Agregue el jamón, las papás picadas y el chorizo picado al potaje. Pique los demás ingredientes en pedacitos chiquitos y sofríalo en aceite de oliva. Agregue el sofrito al potaje. Cocinelo a fuego lento hasta que este un poco espeso. Cocinelo aproximadamente 20 minutos. Añadale sal al gusto.

Da 6-8 raciones.

Rice and Beans
(Moros y Cristianos)

½ lb. black beans *(frijoles negros)*
5 cups water *(agua)*
2 bell peppers *(ají)*
½ lb. bacon *(tocino)*
¼ cup olive oil *(aceite de oliva)*
1 onion *(cebolla)*
3 cloves garlic *(dientes de ajo)*
1 bay leaf *(laurel)*
4 tsps. salt *(sal)*
¼ tsp. oregano *(orégano)*
1 lb. rice *(arroz)*

Place the beans, water and one bell pepper in the pressure cooker for 20 minutes on medium heat. Allow pressure cooker to cool prior to opening. Remove three cups of water from the beans and set aside. Cut the bacon into small squares and sauté until the bacon is crispy. Remove the bacon and sauté bell pepper, onion, garlic, salt, oregano, and bay leaf in olive oil on medium heat. Add raw rice and stir-fry with the sauté for several minutes. Cook on medium heat the rice, sautéed ingredients, beans and the three cups of bean water until the rice is tender.

Serves 6-8.

En un olla de presión, cocine los frijoles, agua y ají en fuego mediano por 20 minutos. Cuele los frijoles y separe tres tazas del agua del frijol. Corte el tocino en trocitos y sofrialo hasta que este tostadito. Remueva la grasa del tocino y añadale los demás ingredientes incluyendo el aceite de oliva. Añadale el arroz crudo y revuelva por unos minutos. Mezcle todo los ingredientes, los frijoles y las tres tazas del agua de frijol y cocine a fuego mediano hasta que el arroz este suave.

Da 6-8 raciones.

Desserts
(Postres)

Custard (Natilla)

Flan (Flan)

Rice Pudding (Arroz con Leche)

These desserts may accompany any dish.
Estos postres se pueden acompañar con cualquier plato.

Custard
(Natilla)

8 egg yolks *(yemas de huevos)*
1 tsp. vanilla extract *(vainilla)*
¼ tsp. salt *(sal)*
4 cups milk *(leche de vaca)*
1½ cup sugar *(azúcar)*
1 cinnamon stick *(ramita de canela)*
1 piece lemon rind *(cáscara de limón)*
4 tsps. corn starch *(maicena)*
¼ cup water *(agua)*
Cinnamon powder *(canela en polvo)*

Boil the milk, cinnamon stick, lemon rind and salt. Set aside. Whip the egg yolks, sugar and corn starch (dissolved in the water). Add the milk to the egg yolk mixture and cook at medium heat, stirring constantly until it thickens. Add the vanilla and stir. Pour into the serving dish and let cool. Sprinkle cinnamon powder over the custard.

Serves 6-8.

Hierva la leche con la canela, sal y cáscara de limón por unos minutos y dejela refrescar. Bata las yemas de los huevos con la azúcar y la maicena disuelta en el agua. Añadale la leche. Cuelelo todo y cocinela a fuego mediano revolviendo constantemente hasta que se espese. Añadale la vainilla y revuelva. Viertala en la dulcera y dejela enfriar bien. Polvoreela con canela y sirvala fria.

Da 6-8 raciones.

Flan
(Flan)

8 eggs *(huevos)*
1 can evaporated milk *(leche evaporada)*
1 can condensed milk *(leche condensada)*
1 tsp. vanilla extract *(vainilla)*
⅛ tsp. salt *(sal)*
1 large cream cheese *(queso crema grande)*
1 cup milk *(leche de vaca)*
½ cup sugar *(azúcar)*

Combine the sugar and some water in a bread loaf pan. Cook over medium heat to form the caramel. Once the sugar has darkened (make sure that the caramel does not burn), the caramel is formed. Set aside. In a blender, mix the remaining ingredients except the evaporated milk. Pour mixture in a bowl and slowly stir in the evaporated milk. Preheat oven to 325 degrees. Pour the mixture over the caramel in the pan and place the flan pan in a pan filled with water. Cook in the oven at 325 degrees for one hour. Remove the flan pan and refrigerate. Once the flan is cool, flip the flan onto a plate and remove from the pan. The caramel will cascade on top of the flan. Slice and serve cold.

Serves 6-8.

Ponga al fuego la media taza de azúcar hasta que se derrita y bañe con ese caramelo un molde de flan. En una batidora, bata los demás ingredientes excepto la leche evaporada. Agregue en una fuente el líquido y revuelva lentamente la leche evaporada. Agregue el líquido en el molde de caramelo. Cocine por una hora en el horno a 325 grados en baño maría. Después que este el flan, metalo a la nevera. Cuando este frio el flan voltelo en un plato con el caramelo encima. Corte y sirvalo frio.

Da 6-8 raciones.

Rice Pudding
(Arroz Con Leche)

½ cup short grain rice *(arroz valencia)*
2½ cups water *(agua)*
1 cinnamon stick *(rama de canela)*
1 piece lemon rind *(pedazo de cáscara de limón)*
1 can evaporated milk *(leche evaporada)*
2 cans condensed milk *(leche condensada)*
1 tbsp. vanilla extract *(vainilla)*
½ tsp. salt *(sal)*
1 large cream cheese *(queso crema grande)*
4 cups whole milk *(leche de vaca)*
Cinnamon powder *(canela en polvo)*

Over medium heat, cook rice, 2½ cups of water, salt, cinnamon stick, and lemon rind for approximately twenty minutes until the rice is soft. Add the whole milk and continue cooking. Stir continuously with a wooden spoon to keep the mixture from sticking to the bottom. Add the condensed and evaporated milk and continue cooking on medium heat and stirring until the mixture thickens and becomes creamy. Cook for approximately one hour. Once it's creamy, add the vanilla extract and stir. Pour the mixture in a serving dish and sprinkle with cinnamon powder. Refrigerate and serve cold.

Serves 8.

Ponga a fuego mediano el arroz, las 2 ½ tazas de agua, la sal, la rama de canela, y la cáscara de limón por aproximadamente veinte minutos hasta que el arroz este blando. Añadale la leche de vaca, continue a cocinarlo en fuego lento y revuelvalo de vez en cuando para que no se pegue en el fondo. Añadale la leche condensada y la leche evaporada y continue revolviendo en fuego mediano hasta que se espese aproximadamente una hora. Después que espese añadale la vainilla. Viertalo en la dulcera y polvoreelo con canela. Pongalo en la nevera y sirvalo frio.

Da 8 raciones.

Coffee
(Café')

Cuban Espresso Coffee (Café Cubano)

Coffee with Milk (Café con Leche)

Espresso with Milk (Cortadito)

Cuban Coffee is a must after every scrumptious meal. Cortadito is best served in the afternoon.
El café Cubano es lo primordial después de una comida sabrosa.
El cortadito se puede servir en la tarde de merienda.

Cuban Expresso Coffee
(Café Cubano)

Finely ground dark roasted coffee
   (grano fino de café oscuro)
4 tsps. sugar *(azúcar)*

You can brew finely ground dark roasted coffee or already ground Cuban blend that comes in a coffee can (can be purchased at most grocery stores in the International aisle). Brew the coffee, and with the first few drips, mix in the sugar and stir until the sugar becomes creamy. Pour in the remainder of the brewed coffee and stir. Serve in demitasse cups.

Serves 6.

Puede colar granos finos de café oscuro o grano fino de café cubano que ya esta en la lata (se compra en el super). Cuele el café y con las primera gotas de café revuelva la azúcar hasta que la azúcar este cremosa. Agregue el resto del café y sirva en tacitas demitasse.

Da 6 raciones.

Café con Leche
(Café con Leche)

Finely ground dark roasted coffee
(grano fino de café oscuro)
4 tsps. sugar *(azúcar)*
Steamed milk *(leche hervida)*
Sugar to taste *(azúcar al gusto)*

You can brew finely ground dark roasted coffee or already ground Cuban blend that comes in a coffee can (can be purchased at most grocery stores in the International aisle). Brew the coffee, and with the first few drips, mix in the 4 tsps. sugar and stir until the sugar becomes creamy. Pour in the remainder of the brewed coffee and stir. In a coffee cup, pour $\frac{1}{3}$ coffee and $\frac{2}{3}$ steamed milk. Add sugar to taste.

Serves 6.

Puede colar granos finos de café oscuro o grano fino de café cubano que ya esta en la lata (se compra en el super). Cuele el café y con las primera gotas de café revuelva las 4 cucharaditas de azúcar hasta que la azúcar este cremosa. Agregue el resto del café. En una taza de café, combine 1/3 de la taza de café con 2/3 de la taza de leche hervida. Añadele azúcar al gusto.

Da 6 raciones.

Cortadito
(Cortadito)

Finely ground dark roasted coffee
   (grano fino de café oscuro)
4 tsps. of sugar *(azúcar)*
Steamed milk *(leche hervida)*
Sugar to taste *(azúcar al gusto)*

You can brew finely ground dark roasted coffee or an already ground Cuban blend that comes in a coffee can (can be purchased at most grocery stores in the International aisle). Brew the coffee and with the first few drips, mix in the 4 tsps. of sugar and stir until the sugar becomes creamy. Pour in the remainder of the brewed coffee and stir. In a small coffee cup, pour ½ coffee and ½ steamed milk. Add sugar to taste.

Serves 6.

Puede colar granos finos de café oscuro o grano fino de café cubano que ya esta en la lata (se compra en el super). Cuele el café y con las primera gotas de café revuelva las 4 cucharaditas de azúcar hasta que la azúcar este cremosa. Agregue el resto del café. En una taza de café pequeña, combine ½ taza de café con ½ taza de leche hervida. Añadale azúcar al gusto.

Da 6 raciones.

Author's Biography

Yolanda Natividad Perez, known to her family and friends as Yoly, was born in Havana, Cuba on December 25, 1964. The Communist take-over caused her family to leave Cuba when she was three.

As with so many other Cuban families, the hardships and challenges of beginning again in a new democratic country created close, positive and loving ties to both the lives they live today, and the heritage they carry with them.

She is a practicing Architect/Designer living in Houston and practicing throughout the United States and Latin America. Love for cooking, her affection for her grandmother, and her desire to pass on these family recipes to nieces and nephews who would never know first-hand the richness of Café Mima's cooking, led her to compile this cookbook.

Writing this book, has enabled her to tap into the peace and warmth of those childhood memories of tastes, scents, and sounds of her grandmother's loving kitchen. And she trusts that the creation, design, and offering of this book come straight from both of their hearts.

Buen Provecho!! (Enjoy your meal!!)

Biografía del Autor

Yolanda Natividad Pérez, conocida en su familia y amistades como Yoly, nació el 25 de Diciembre de 1964 en la Havana, Cuba. Al tomar el poder el Comunismo, su familia se fué de Cuba cuando ella tenía tres años de edad.

Como muchas otras familias Cubanas, el sufrimiento y desafío de empezar otra vez en un nuevo país, creo una unión y un apego especial que viven hoy y que será una herencia que llevarán con ellos para siempre.

Ella es una Arquitecta/Diseñadora que vive en Houston y ejerce su carrera en los Estados Unidos y Latino America. Su amor por la cocina, su cariño por su Abuela y el deseo de transmitirles estas recetas familiares a su sobrina y sus sobrinos que nunca sabrán la delicia de la comida de Café Mima, la inspiró a escribir este libro.

Ella cuenta que el escribir éste libro le dio mucha paz y nostalgia el recordar las memorias de los olores, sonidos y sabores de la cocina tan acojedora de su Abuela. Ella confía que la creación, diseño y compartimiento de este libro viene directamente del corazón de ambas.

Buen Provecho!!

Café Mima Cuban Cookbook Order Form

Name _____

Address _____

City _____ State _____ Zip _____

Telephone _____ Email _____

Café Mima Cuban Cookbook — $21.95 per copy plus $4.00 handling and postage per book.

Make checks or money orders payable to *Café Mima Cuban Cookbook* and mail to:

Café Mima Cuban Cookbook
1449 Fountain View
Houston, Texas 77056

Texas residents, also add applicable state sales tax.

Quantity	Price	Total

Subtotal _____

Sales Tax (*TX only*) _____

Shipping ____ **$4.00** _____

TOTAL _____

Thank you for your order. Enjoy!